PORTFOLIO L

METROPOLITAN SEMINARS IN ART

Great Periods in Painting

PORTFOLIO L

Actaeon and the Atom

ART IN THE CONTEMPORARY WORLD

BY JOHN CANADAY

ART EDITOR AND CRITIC
THE NEW YORK TIMES

THE METROPOLITAN MUSEUM OF ART

ACTAEON AND THE ATOM
Art in the Contemporary World

ACCORDING to classical legend the hunter Actaeon surprised the goddess Diana bathing in a forest pool. As punishment he was turned into a stag, chased down by his own hounds, and killed. The title of our concluding discussion, Actaeon and the Atom, was suggested by the poem "Science" by Robinson Jeffers. The implication is that man, having looked upon the atom, may for his temerity suffer a fate similar to Actaeon's.

What has this to do with art? Some people have found a connection in pictures like Picasso's cubist *Man with Violin* (*Figure 1*). Painted in 1911, it is a shifting pattern of geometrical shapes that merge, overlap, and break against one another, revealing only here and there some recognizable element of a human figure or a musical instrument. Its title tells us that the painter began with a subject involving only simple and familiar objects, although he ended by destroying them. (For what reason, we will see later.)

Certainly when Picasso painted *Man with Violin* he had no intention of offering us an analogy to atomic research. But since then the cubist way of breaking and shattering form has been compared to the dissolution of matter brought about by man's discovery of atomic structure and the means of its disruption. Call it only coincidence that the scientist and the painter were simultaneously carrying on research that ended in comparable results in the laboratory and the studio—but the coincidence remains a startling one.

Art has always expressed ideas basic to its time, occasionally by intention but more often simply because the artist responds to what is in the air. At times the artist, as a kind of prophet without prophetic intention, has even anticipated the general nature of events to come. Critics not too concerned with caution have seen in cubist pictures like *Man with Violin* a prophecy of the atomic bomb—an interesting idea whether or not a tenable one.

In another way the art of the twentieth century suggests a shattered age: artists seem to work in a multitude of contradictory styles without focus or direction, whereas the artists of the past seem, in retrospect, to have made unified progress toward a goal. The color plates and the other illustrations in this portfolio must look like a hodgepodge in comparison with those in our discussions of other centuries—even the nineteenth, with all its variety. One reason is our lack of perspective at such close range; another is that the art of our time is, just as it appears to be, more various than that of any other. The artist has hundreds of sources of inspiration—travel, museums, and the color reproductions that have brought the art of the past and of far-away places into the painter's studio. A painter living today in, say, Utah may have a wider acquaintance with the art of renaissance Italy than he might have had had he lived in one of the minor capitals of renaissance Italy itself. In addition the renaissance artist was ignorant of vast fields of art that have tre-

Figure 1

mendously influenced modern art. He knew nothing of the art of China, of Japan, of ancient Mexico, of Egypt, of half a dozen other civilizations. For that matter he had only a limited and inaccurate acquaintance with the art of ancient Greece, in spite of the revival of classicism. Even the artists who lived in renaissance Rome knew less about the ancient city than we do with our advantage of several additional centuries of excavation and study.

This richness of reference material has been both good and bad for modern artists. It has been bad when they have tried to imitate the arts of past civilizations without understanding the thought and the life that produced them. The multiplicity of beautiful forms has stunted many creative talents by leading artists into imitation rather than invention. On the other hand, Picasso remains the most inventive painter of our century even when he refers directly to the past, as in *Mother and Child* (Plate L1), where the forms of classicism serve as a point of departure for a composition that could be the product only of our own century.

Artist and Public

It is not surprising that with such diversity the work of many artists is incomprehensible. The general public understands art that it can relate to what it already knows, believes, feels. And since we as individuals can be familiar with only a small part of what there is to be known and felt, there are large fields of contemporary art that lie outside our ken.

The situation is further complicated in that our age has produced the artist who works only to please himself, to express his inmost feelings and convictions for his own satisfaction rather than for an audience—an approach to painting that is peculiar to our time. We saw that to some extent Van Gogh worked in this way: his painting was a release of his own spiritual turmoil and was incomprehensible to the public of his day because the form of ex-

pression was new. Today the same thing happens on an exaggerated scale when an artist paints in a way so extremely personal that he uses a kind of private vocabulary, leaving the average observer at a loss as to how to approach an understanding of his painting.

Can we organize this chaotic material into convenient categories? Our early portfolios Expressionism and Abstraction were essentially discussions of two large categories of modern art, although we also referred to old masters. And in the concluding discussions of the first series, The Artist as a Social Critic and The Artist as a Visionary, we also included many contemporary painters. The plates in those four portfolios might be reviewed as a beginning to this discussion; a few of them will be referred to specifically. A broad treatment, rather than a detailed survey condensed to names and dates, will serve us best and will enable us to relate to realism, abstraction, expressionism, social statement, and fantasy.

Modern Realism

In the first place, let us say that although "modern art" is usually taken to mean the more extreme abstract art so much publicized at the moment, an over-all view of the century shows that this emphasis is exaggerated. Although realism has been discarded by the majority of contemporary painters whose names are most conspicuous (partly because they make the liveliest copy for magazine and newspaper stories), realism has not died. It is a more significant force than is indicated by the bulk of art criticism, which naturally concerns itself with innovations.

If we except Russia, where a routine, pedestrian realism is dictated by the state, we find the realistic tradition flourishing most vigorously in the United States. Americans have been in the forefront of the movement that has produced the most extreme forms of abstract art during the last ten years, but be-

Figure 2

neath this agitated surface there has been a sound and steady continuation of traditional forms.

A deliberate return to realism occurred in the 1930s when a group of Americans specifically and emphatically rejected European modernisms and dedicated themselves to American subject matter and traditions. These men painted largely in the Middle West, the geographical heart of the nation and, they liked to believe, its spiritual heart also. They acquired the name of regionalists. The movement had its adherents in the Far West also and even in New York City where Reginald Marsh (1898–1954) and his followers devoted themselves to the small area of Manhattan Island (*Figure 2*). But regionalism means Middle Westernism generally, and its trio of big names was John Steuart Curry (1897–1946), Thomas Hart Benton (born 1889), and Grant Wood (1892–1942).

For a few years one heard more about them than about any other American artists. But their movement died, or at least went into eclipse—in part because it exhausted itself within self-imposed limitations, in part because the Second World War showed us that the United States could not isolate itself within its national boundaries, much less within the boundaries of Missouri, Kansas, and Iowa, where regionalism was most avidly cultivated.

American Gothic

The best-known regionalist painting is still the one that was best known during the movement's heyday, Grant Wood's *American Gothic* (Plate L2), which made the painter famous overnight. The picture was appealing on several scores. Its precise, polished technique was a welcome relief from the technical abandon of much painting of the time. Also its subject matter was fresh. The rickrack braid, the gingham dress, the pitchfork, the "Gothic" farmhouse, the severe, unlovely faces of the man and woman—none of these had been capitalized upon as material for painting; they came as novelties.

But this most enduring regionalist picture has less to do with the idealism of "the heart of America" than with semisatirical comment. It echoes the social criticism that Sinclair Lewis in *Main Street* and Sherwood Anderson in *Winesburg, Ohio* directed toward the American small town, finding in it less natural nobility than bigotry, prejudice, repression, and intellectual limitation. Although the farmer and his wife are represented as sturdy folk of high moral principles, *American Gothic* also speaks of provincial, unreceptive narrowness.

Benton and Curry

Thomas Hart Benton, bearing a family name distinguished in Middle Western politics, painted for a while in Europe, experimenting with modern movements, but upon his return to this country he reacted against European painting and became a proselytizer for the

8

American scene and for its native arts. Every backwoods or provincial American activity from the manufacture and consumption of moonshine to hillbilly music, just coming into its own at that time as a folk art of interest to intellectuals, fascinated him. Every picturesque locale from river port to boom town (*Figure 3*) offered material. His reputation has suffered even more than that of the school in general, and the artificiality of his style seems out of key with the folksiness of his subjects, leaving us with the feeling that although he wanted to get to the heart of his material, he managed only to observe it from the outside and record it inappropriately.

The third member of the regionalist hierarchy was John Steuart Curry, who of the three was most impressed with the richness, the energy of the Middle Western earth. His *Wisconsin Landscape* (*Figure 4*) is less well known than Wood's *American Gothic*, but it may prove to be a better summary of the regionalist ideal in the broad sweep of the landscape, its lushness, the idealization of the earth's fertility turned to the nation's service.

The Mexicans

The regionalists found their point of departure in the ideas of a group of painters who some-

Figure 3

9

Figure 4

what earlier had turned from Europeanisms to the celebration of their own country's history and hopes: the painters of the Mexican Renaissance. More didactic than the Americans, they covered the walls of public buildings with frescoes as a means of visual education for the mass of people just emerging from illiteracy, suppression, and exploitation. We have seen *Sugar Cane* and *The Liberation of the Peon* (Portfolio 8, Plates 95, 96; Portfolio 11, Plate 128) by Diego Rivera (1886–1957), the dean of the school, who abandoned an early career as a cubist and evolved his style from the massive forms of sculpture native to Mexico in the pre-Columbian centuries.

Rivera's reputation has tobogganed almost as drastically as that of the Middle Westerners, although there are signs of a revival. But that of his colleague José Clemente Orozco (1883–1949) has more than held its own. Rivera, like Benton, became too dependent on a formula that grew tiresome or at best only decorative. Orozco's art has endured because although he dedicated it to social statement, at first dealing specifically with the Mexican struggle for freedom and enlightenment, he generalized his themes. *Barricade* (*Figure 5*),

for example, may have had its origin in the Mexican uprising by which the common people won the land from the rich landlords, but it holds its own as an expression of violent struggle toward an ideal. It is, of course, expressionist in style, which has taken us into a detour from the subject of realism.

Wyeth and Pollock

Realism was adopted by the regionalists as an appropriate device for the service of a cause. What about realism—today—as a means of personal expression, as opposed to the eccentric, individual styles that many feel enable a painter to express his most intimate self?

Today we find no organized school, no group of painters devoted to its propagation and defense. We find instead individual painters who speak through realistic images. Usually, we must admit, they speak without much imagination, giving support to the idea that abstract expressions are most sympathetic to our time. But there are exceptions. One, indicating the continued legitimacy and vigor of the realistic image, is the American Andrew Wyeth (born 1917).

Wyeth is not concerned with social or political theories. He has no drum to beat. He is a traditional painter who regards painting as a personal expression to be shared as clearly and as intimately as possible with the observer. The world that interests him is not limited by national boundaries or by current events or by philosophies popular at any one time. He happens to choose his subjects from the northeastern section of the country—since he lives there. But his world is the world of nature, and of people in it, a world that may be pondered by all men at all times. His own vision of it is poetic, thoughtful, and in the end serene, in spite of the intensity of his feeling.

River Cove (Plate L 3), which Wyeth painted in 1958, is composed of elements that would be commonplace or meaningless in the hands of a purely imitative realist. The picture does seem to imitate down to the last detail various familiar elements of nature—a bit of river, a sand bank running into it and discernible not only where it rises from the water but where it is submerged. The water, the sand with its shells and tracks of a heron, and a band of trees along the bank—unseen but reflected in the water—are the picture's simple components. Yet all are invested with an enchantment that recalls our first experiences of nature, the revelation that comes to us when, usually in adolescence, we first see the world not as something to be taken for granted, but as part of a miracle beyond explanation, existing all around us.

The sensation of enchantment and the miraculous produced by *River Cove* is explainable largely by the fact that every detail, down to the last broken shell or bit of gravel, is revealed in acute, more-than-real clarity. Condensed within the boundaries of a picture, these details are apparent to us as they would not be in nature if we were at sufficient distance to encompass the same field of vision. It is as if we were gifted with supernatural sight or as if the air between us and the objects were a lens, sharpening and revealing every detail.

From such a description, we might believe that to produce such an effect the artist need only master the technique of accurate draughtsmanship and smooth painting, then select a subject and reproduce it. But of course *River Cove* is a fine picture not because the artist is a superb technician but because his technique is the proper means to his expressive end. The multitudinous details of *River Cove* are organized into a few large, simple harmonious areas conveying the peace, the serenity, the deep and eternal life of nature. Without such organization the picture would be nothing more than an accumulation of sharply painted details without meaning, even without interest beyond their display of technical skill. In the end the picture depends upon the artist's innate response to his subject and upon his inmost emotional capacity for that response.

Making a sharp about-face, we may see in *Autumn Rhythm* (Plate L 4) by Jackson Pollock (1912–1956) a contrasting way of expressing this "inmost emotional capacity." The title indicates that this painting, like *River Cove*, was

Figure 5

Figure 6

inspired by a response to nature. But any effort to discover in *Autumn Rhythm* such forms as trees, clouds, and streams is to defeat the artist's purpose. A huge canvas, seventeen feet long, *Autumn Rhythm* was painted by flinging, dripping, and flicking liquid paint onto a canvas stretched flat on the floor.

This form of abstract expressionism is sometimes called action painting. Since the actual physical movements of the painter are reflected in the shape of the forms that he gives us so directly, we should feel closer to Pollock than to Wyeth. The rush of Pollock's attack, which places a minimum of technical interruption between the painter and what he paints, is relayed to us. We feel the painter's presence as we feel the presence of a person in his handwriting. *Autumn Rhythm* and pictures of its kind are indeed executed in a kind of handwriting, although the language and the written symbols do not translate into familiar terms.

By simplest explanation, *Autumn Rhythm* tells us how Pollock responds to what must

be called his subject, just as a Van Gogh, with its broad strokes and its gobbets of paint, tells us how that artist feels about his. And theoretically there should be less difficulty in identifying ourselves with Pollock because we are not inhibited by our own conditioned responses to any recognizable objects. In other words, a Van Gogh or a Wyeth, while not at all similar, are both pictures of subjects to which we have our own reaction and to which the artists have theirs. Our response to their pictures is a mixture of our own already established ideas and theirs. But in the Pollock our response should be entirely that of the artist. The idea of the artist as a being gifted with special responses and the ability to give them visual form here reaches its ultimate statement.

Pollock, who was killed at the height of his career in an automobile accident in 1956, is already the old master of the school of abstract expressionism—by definition, the school of painting that depends on the emotional impact of color and shape alone, without image, to relay the painter's sensations. Willem de Kooning (born 1904) among living abstract expressionists probably holds the lead in a field that has become so fashionable that sincere and competent artists are all but smothered by a crowd of charlatans at worst and incompetents at best. De Kooning works on large canvases in a broad, slashing style (*Figure 6*), and his effects are hopefully imitated by hundreds of painters all over this country as well as in Europe.

Many people will enjoy Pollock and De Kooning only for their patterns and color, just as many people will enjoy Wyeth only because he paints a "picture of something," missing in both cases the special and personal interpretative talent of the artist. Which artist is on the right track? Is it Wyeth, who follows a road in a direction that has been set for centuries, yet continues to find it the best route to expression? Or is it Pollock's descendants who think that the road has long since reached its end and who have cut off into uncharted country to discover what they can? The nearest thing to an answer may be suggested by the fact that in many art collections paintings by Pollock and Wyeth are equally honored, and equally enjoyed by their owners.

But to confuse things, one school of abstract painters objects as strenuously to the autographic, free-flowing, hard-hitting styles of abstract expressionism as it does to realism. These painters insist instead upon a rigidly controlled geometrical pattern, with Piet Mondrian (Portfolio 4, Plates 41, 42, 43, *Figures 8–14*) as their idol, with his self-limited use of black horizontal and vertical lines against white, plus areas of flat red, yellow, or blue.

Again, Romantic and Classic

Where did all this variety come from? The ancestry of modern art is long and compli-

Figure 8

Figure 7

cated. We could follow De Kooning, Pollock, and their fellows back not only to Van Gogh but through Delacroix to Rubens—to mention only a few of the most important figures—in tracing a romantic tradition of color and movement and almost compulsive individualism. And Pollock's gobbets and rivulets of color have a direct and acknowledged ancestor in the broken strokes of Monet's late impressionist works. Or the tradition of Mondrian could be traced back through Seurat to Poussin—the classical tradition of discipline, repose, and intellectualism rather than emotionalism, of restraint rather than release.

As for the immediate background, in our last discussion we saw Cézanne and Seurat as the postimpressionist masters of the classical tradition, Van Gogh and Gauguin of the romantic one. The last two were direct sources for the school of expressionism—not yet abstract—that flourished in Germany in several forms from the years just before the First World War until the advent of Hitler (who outlawed expressionist painting as degenerate).

Expressionism was concerned with intense emotions, and it used intense means to convey these emotions. We have seen enough examples, beginning in Portfolio 3 on the general subject of expressionism, to make two more sufficient. The portrait of a man (*Figure 7*) by Erich Heckel (born 1883), which if not a portrait of the painter in fact is at least one in spirit, has all the ingrown, rather morbid but personal and moving quality of the early school. And the city street (*Figure 8*) that George Grosz (1893–1959) diagrams as a concentration of evil and misery shows expressionism after it turned away from personal reveries or fears to delineate some of the horror of a time that had produced one

ghastly war and was soon to produce another. The intentional ugliness of the line, from which all suavity and grace has been removed, does as much as the subject to reveal the brutality and viciousness, the sinister menace, of a corroded civilization.

In view of these examples, with their emphasis on subject, it is surprising that the first completely abstract painting was done about 1910 by a man who had been associated with expressionism in an early phase: Wassily Kandinsky (1866–1944), whose *Black Lines*, with its obvious relationship to contemporary abstract expressionism, we have already seen (Portfolio 4, Plate 44). But Kandinsky also created compositions such as *Geometrical Forms* (*Figure 9*) that are equally related to the opposing branch of abstraction that, by stretching a point, we have called "classical."

Fauvism

In France the expressionist impulse produced a happier movement called fauvism. Referring more to Gauguin than to Van Gogh (who after all was a northerner, and more appealing to German emotionalism than to the French), the fauves found their leader in Henri Matisse, already familiar in these discussions through his *Lady in Blue* (Portfolio 5, Plate 51).

A fauve is by literal translation a wild beast. The name was given in derision, and few names could have been more inappropriate for a group of highly civilized painters whose art has become an adjunct to elegant living. Matisse's early *Pink Onions* (Plate L 5) may explain, however, why this art of civilized nuance seemed barbarous fifty years ago. Not only the art of Gauguin with its flat, ornamental color areas, but the art of children is reflected here. Struck by the freshness and immediacy of children's art (now generally appreciated, but then dismissed without much thought), Matisse incorporated elements of it in *Pink Onions*, notably in the border of unpainted canvas around the objects and in the

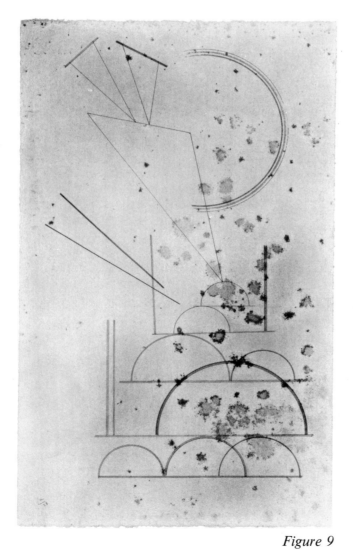

Figure 9

14

31/60

Georges Rouault

15

quick, improvisational character of the whole.

Matisse's improvisation is of course not the result of technical innocence, but of a high degree of training and sophistication. The colors and the arrangement of *Pink Onions* are dependent upon knowledge and theory of color and form relationships in spite of the fact that they seem to have been improvised on the spur of the moment.

In a long career Matisse investigated a variety of methods and theories, but he always believed that painting is an art of handsome color in which the effect of spontaneity is important. This idea was propounded by Delacroix and followed to a large degree by Renoir, which places Matisse in a tradition thoroughly and delightfully French.

Fauvism was never an organized movement, but rather a fortuitous temporary conjunction of young painters who shared similar interests. As a group they soon dissolved, some of them, like Raoul Dufy, developing a lighthearted manner capitalizing on the most seductive aspects of fauvism, while others, notably Georges Rouault (1871–1958), emphasized an emotional mysticism closer to German expressionism (*Figure 10*).

We have begun to give the impression, no doubt, that any twentieth-century painter can be placed in one pigeonhole or another. But this is true only if we keep our definitions elastic. It also depends on a point of view. Franklin Watkins (born 1894), one of the deans of American painting, came into prominence in 1931 when he won the Carnegie International award for his *Suicide in Costume* (*Figure 11*). Certainly it is easy enough to find expressionist elements in the picture, with its twisted, agonized forms. But it is also a fantasy with symbolic content. Watkins' much later *Still Life* (Plate L6) has retained some expressionist feeling in its mild distortions, yet a violent addict of abstract expressionism would consider it virtually realistic, while an extremely conservative painter on the other hand might regret such departures from visual fact

as the artist has made. The combination of objects has, no doubt, some kind of personal symbolism that the painter does not explain; in addition the picture is a tightly organized composition that could suggest a study of some of Cézanne's principles. It is, in short, a completely unclassifiable picture by a painter of much talent and experience who has been nourished from many sources without following any one school, subjecting all influences to his own vision. As the experiments of the first half of our century have been absorbed into our experience, they have become part of the fabric of traditional painting.

Cubism

The influence of expressionism, including fauvism, was tremendous but not quite as spectacular and not as completely revolutionary as that of a movement that can still enrage and puzzle museumgoers—cubism. At the conclusion of our last discussion we saw Picasso, in his masklike portrait of Gertrude Stein (Plate K12), suddenly influenced by the tribal art of Africa.

It is a paradox, of course, that the art of primitive people should have exerted so strong an influence on the sophisticates and intellectuals of Paris in their search for new forms. It is important to remember that the impact of this art had nothing to do with a return to primitivism, a denial of intellectual values. Quite the reverse. For, although the vigor of the art of primitive peoples, African and other, certainly made its appeal to artists surfeited with the stale academic conventions that were still powerful at the beginning of the century, they did not delude themselves into thinking that they could induce in themselves the state of mind that had created these fascinating objects. What the artists did find in African sculpture were new concepts of form.

At first the form was more or less imitated, or adapted, as in the portrait of Gertrude Stein. The painter Amedeo Modigliani (1884–

1920) developed a style in which the moody spirit and the linear pattern of Botticelli were combined with African elements. Modigliani's *Italian Woman* (Plate L7) can be compared with Botticelli's *Venus* (Plates D1, D2) on the one hand and with African sculpture on the other (Portfolio K, *Figure 20*). Here again we have one of the many personal styles of the first quarter of the century that can be called expressionist in a wide definition of the term. The adaptation of the geometrical forms of African sculpture as exemplified in *Gertrude Stein* and *Italian Woman*, however, did not for long satisfy Picasso or his two fellow artists Georges Braque (born 1882) and Juan Gris (1887–1927), who, with him, first formulated

and put into practice the tenets of cubism.

In its simplest form, cubism is connected not only with the geometry of African sculpture but with Cézanne's statement that all forms in nature can be reduced to the cube, the cylinder, and the sphere. In a picture like *Road near l'Estaque* (*Figure 12*) Braque takes natural forms and reduces them in ways intended either to increase our response to the geometrical foundations of natural objects or to their innate energy.

The most complicating factor in cubism is the device called simultaneity. In *Tea Time* (*Figure 13*) by Jean Metzinger (1883–1956), this device is used in ways obvious enough to make the picture ideal for purposes of explana-

17

Collection Museum of Modern Art

Figure 12

Demoiselles d'Avignon (Portfolio 4, Plate 4) painted in 1907 and often called the first cubist picture. The picture served Picasso as an investigation of new ideas, and its earlier parts at the left side, with their rather static quality, show by contrast with the later ones on the right how the idea of motion and simultaneous vision developed while the work was in progress. It is worth mentioning that Picasso did not exhibit the picture until long after the cubist sensation had waned; accusations that he painted it to create a scandal are thus refuted. But the picture did have a wide influence on cubist development since other artists knew it well from Picasso's studio.

Futurism

In the early days of the development of cubism's complicated theories, an Italian movement called futurism was propounding an overlapping one. The futurist revolution (which never quite came off) was based on what its advocates called dynamism, arguing that in our age of speed, noise, and mechanization the old forms of painting should be abolished for

tion. The teacup in the lower part of the composition is seen from two points of view simultaneously. One half is seen directly head on, the other from slightly above. Since we see the cup in two ways simultaneously, we go beyond the limits of conventional photography and perspective, which show only a single aspect of an object at one time. If we could also see the cup directly from above and from below, and so on, we would have a total image, but here the simultaneity is not pushed that far.

Similarly we see two simultaneous aspects of the woman's face. We see a profile if we disregard the left half of it; looking at the whole, we see the full face. The objection that neither profile nor full face is photographically correct does not hold, since photographic correctness is not the standard. What we see is a pattern of shifting planes that has its own energy, whether or not we like the distortions thus produced of a woman with a teacup.

The desire to portray energy is behind much early cubism; it is certainly present in the lunging, swinging forms of Picasso's celebrated

Figure 13

18

Figure 14

new ones expressive of our civilization. *Dynamism of an Automobile* (*Figure 14*) by Luigi Russolo (born 1885) shows one effort to paint on static canvas changing aspects of a speeding object and the lines of force surrounding it.

But from the first there was something a little forced about the theories of futurism. They sounded fine in print, yet they rang a little hollow when translated into paint. Futurism was essentially a literary movement, in spite of the impressive agitation in some of its paintings and in the sculptural masterpiece of the school, *Unique Forms of Continuity in Space* (*Figure 15*), wherein Umberto Boccioni (1882–1916) achieved the difficult feat of suggesting the movement of a solid object through space, without the advantage of the overlapping and transparent forms that can be represented in painting.

Where futurism failed to achieve its promise, cubism proved capable of absorbing and digesting and expanding. It went through several phases in rapid succession, and since then has affected almost every other movement and has played infinite variations upon itself. After the stage where the object remained recognizable (Braque's *Road near l'Estaque*), the principle of simultaneity was applied in more and more complicated ways. This was the analytical stage, and the term was well chosen. Artists began to analyze form so

thoroughly that eventually the complexity of planes reduced the image to unrecognizability, as in *Man with Violin* with which we opened this discussion. What should have been a total image became no image at all, but the abstract pattern that resulted had its own character, its own attraction both intellectual and decorative, and showed that pure abstraction devoid of image might be an end in itself. This, of course—for good or ill—was of tremendous importance in the development of modern art.

At this point, when cubism could apparently go no farther in the direction of abstraction, it split up into a dozen different branches, all based on geometry and simultaneity but differing in application. Cubism proper abandoned the analytical approach and reverted to one in which the image once again became more or less recognizable. This phase, which produced some of the most attractive works of the movement, is most properly known as synthetic cubism or sometimes, rather appropriately, as decorative cubism.

Figure 15

Cubism and Personal Style

To the beginner, cubist paintings look all alike, but there are distinctive differences between painters. Some early Braques and Picassos of the analytical kind are all but indistinguishable from one another; however, in the freer synthetic phase the personalities of the two men separated their work decisively.

While Picasso ranged far and wide, Braque stuck fairly close to cubist principles, varying them in subtle ways and even incorporating with them some of the coloristic richness of fauvism. His *Woman with a Mandolin* (*Figure 16*) is a masterpiece of harmony between what one would expect to be altogether incompatible approaches.

The Spaniard Juan Gris deserves the title of cubism's poet. Gris always insisted that the image should remain recognizable, should never be analyzed out of existence, and should legitimately carry its association as an object. In his *Place Ravignan* (Plate L8) we discern clearly a table holding a bowl of fruit, the window beyond, and the trees of the square beyond that. The picture is a souvenir of Gris's studio, and one may ask what the artist has gained by departing so far from the natural look of things if he insists that they should retain their recognizability. He has gained a new freedom in composition, one in which he may more arbitrarily build his pictorial structure, may more arbitrarily design his color, may free himself from the natural laws of vision in order to investigate in a new way an old familiar world.

To some people this will seem a doubtful freedom, an escape from one kind of monotonous formula to another. Picasso, the most inventive of the cubists, apparently felt that way—for a while. He reacted against cubist disruption of form and entered his "classical" period, painting the emphatically solid forms of pictures like *Mother and Child*, which we have just seen. We may now see too that the cylindrical and spherical forms of these gigantic, somewhat ponderous classical echoes are also echoes of Cézanne, as if Picasso had decided to take off again from the cubist starting point of "the cube, the cylinder, and the sphere" to discover what lay in another direction.

He soon discovered, however, that the cubist adventure had supplied him with a vocabulary he could not relinquish. The foray into a form of classicism cleared the air for him, and since that time, in a dazzling sequence of manners, he has turned cubist ideas to a variety of purposes, as we have previously seen in *The Studio* (Portfolio 4, Plate 38) and the masterful *Guernica* (Portfolio 6, *Figures 6, 7*).

As one more important variant—among many—we must mention Fernand Léger (1881–1955), who followed some of the early analytical cubist experiments but came into his own with a bright, bold, strongly defined style based on mechanistic elements. Like the futurists (and other groups, for that matter) he believed that since ours is an urban civilization, the painter's richest material is to be found in the city and the mechanisms that dominate it. But where the futurists stressed dynamism, Léger was interested in the sleekness of machine parts, the patterns created by mechanical contrivances as static objects rather than by their motion. In *The City* (Plate L9) he applied this theory not only by choosing city forms as his subject—smokestacks, signboards, girders, and the like—but by reducing these forms to a geometry as smooth as pistons and ball bearings. Even the individuals who inhabit this city have the mechanistic air of robots.

In later work Léger shifted to a curvilinear style, as in *Divers on Yellow Background* (*Figure 17*), but he clung to the smooth, steady motion of the simplified surface, the impersonal character of a well-built machine.

Fantasy: Paul Klee

In what we have seen so far we have been able to distinguish three currents; the social realism

Figure 16

of the Mexicans and the American regionalists, the personal emphasis of expressionism, and the analytical intellectualism of the cubists, all overlapping here and there. But in all of them, singly or as a group, one element is missing or only hinted at occasionally: the element of fantasy, the exploration of the world of mystery and magic, of the supernatural that has always been a realm of the artist. In this realm the Swiss-German Paul Klee occupies a position comparable to that of Picasso in formal analysis and of Matisse in color.

Klee had early associations with German expressionism, and later ones with cubism.

His *Landscape with Bluebirds* (*Figure 18*) holds references to both—to expressionism in its bright, arbitrary color, and to cubism in its angular patterns. It is a fairy-tale landscape, naïve on the surface, infinitely sophisticated in fact. His *Letter Ghost* (*Figure 19*) seems simpler, but is even more subtle. The picture is what we call a pictorial pun; the head and shoulders of the ghost are formed from the shapes of the flaps of the back of an ordinary envelope, transformed by a few lines into an eerie image. It is worth reminding ourselves here that African masks interested Picasso and Matisse as geometrical forms offering clues to

Figure 17

Figure 18

new techniques of pictorial construction. But Klee was interested rather in the spirit of incantation that they evoked. Primitive art is concerned with superstition and sorcery, and while Klee had no more desire than Picasso or Matisse to revert to the state of mind of a savage, he found in primitive art forms a door to a world of fancy that is hidden from most of us by the hard facts of the world around us.

In the art of children he found another door. We saw that Matisse in *Pink Onions* was interested in the spontaneous effect and the technical devices of children's painting. Klee was interested in the world that children reveal in their painting, a world of innocence and of direct vision unencumbered by the deadening overlay of what we call practical common

sense that life imposes on us. Even in the art of the insane, Klee found expression of an inner, secret world, which is ordinarily concealed.

All this explains why *Landscape with Blue-*

Figure 19

Figure 20

birds, *Letter Ghost*, and *Demon as Pirate* (Portfolio 12, Plate 143) have a deceptive resemblance to the art of innocents or irrational people, though they are in fact the work of a sensitive and trained intellect. If *Letter Ghost* were nothing more than a trick, or as we have called it, a pictorial pun, it would be only amusing. But it is surely impossible to deny that the mysterious and even menacing figure imposes itself upon us more and more strongly each time we look at it, until it takes on a haunting power.

Klee worked in a variety of ways. Sometimes his work is completely abstract; sometimes a canvas will contain cryptic scribbles like the marks of tribal tattoo or the cabalistic symbols of voodoo. His pictures are usually small; sometimes they are extremely lighthearted, sometimes threatening. One of his largest pictures, and one of his most complicated compositions, is *Fish Magic* (Plate L10). It is also one in which the symbolism is important. At the risk of making a more exact translation of these symbols than Klee had in mind, we can at least uncover the general nature of the picture's theme.

Fish Magic is bright and happy enough for a kindergarten, but its theme is philosophical. Time, first symbolized by the clock, is suspended in the center of the picture within lines which suggest at once a tower and a trap. The sun and moon, which circle in time, are represented nearby, while around and about is a luminous pattern of flowers—symbol of transience—and fish—symbol of time backward into primeval darkness and, by extension of early Christian iconography, of time forward into eternity. In the lower right a bouquet has been placed in a goblet of water, but the futility of this effort to modify time is apparent when we notice that the very goblet takes on the shape of an hourglass. Near the goblet stands a little figure whose face exists doubly. Of his two mouths, one is shaped like a heart, symbol of man's emotional and intuitive nature; the other is an arithmetical symbol.

These antitheses coexist in man, and man exists in time, which exists doubly as the moment and as eternity, which are indivisible. The little figure expounds this lesson, and the kindergarten picture becomes a symbol of the universe, which—an encouraging exception in our century—the artist finds in order.

Chagall

Klee, then, is an extremely complicated artist. He is also an artist who will not appeal to everybody, even though most critics today regard him as a giant of modern art. A fantasist of different spirit, and more immediate appeal, is the Russian Marc Chagall (born 1889).

Chagall went to Paris in his early twenties, and was at first much affected by the experimental painters at work there. His *The Poet, or Half Past Three* (*Figure 20*) was painted in 1911, when cubism and fauvism had established new directions. In *The Poet* there are obvious cubist elements apparent in the angularities and the overlapping and broken planes of objects. But in its color, which is very bright and fresh, it is fauvist. Ultimately it is neither cubist nor fauvist, but a playful fantasy in which we may imagine that the poet's head is put upside down on his shoulders not for any reasons of cubist theory but because poets, being curious people, see things differently from the rest of us.

Before long Chagall abandoned all but the most superficial use of cubist, fauvist, or other experimental principles and began painting his own dreamworld: a very happy place peopled by flowers, lovers, and engaging animals who had, so to speak, accompanied him to France from the Russian farm villages he had known as a boy.

Bouquet with Flying Lovers (Plate L11) is a typical Chagall fantasy in its singing color, its flowers, its floating figures (for Chagall's lovers are as likely to fly as to walk, as likely to stand on their heads as on their feet), and in its echoes of a benignly Bohemian way of

25

life. The simple interior in the left half of the composition merges with the river, bridge, and houses that perhaps might be seen from its windows. A jolly cowlike creature, with a body resembling a violin, appears in the upper left, and an unexplained but friendly giant of a rooster looms over the horizon.

In Chagall's delightful visions, absurdity is never questioned. It is accepted as part of a warm and carefree world whose inhabitants need only one another, some flowers, and the rich colors of things around them as the components of a very special paradise.

Dadaism

The real world in which Chagall painted, however, was not at all a paradise, and it held absurdities that were sinister rather than engaging. If his art was a revolt against intellectualism, the explanation was simply that he was one of those romantics who make their own world from the richness of their own spirit; in Chagall's case a happy spirit. In contrast, just after the First World War there arose a different kind of reaction against intellectualism in art and the cultivation of a different kind of absurdity, as bizarre a development as the history of art offers. This was the movement descriptively called dada.

Dada was a deliberate rejection of the rational bases of art, a sort of desperate and shocking clowning that produced such wildly nonsensical items as *Why Not Sneeze, Rose*

Figure 21

Figure 22

Sélavy? (*Figure 21*) by Marcel Duchamp (born 1887). As a product of the deranged times that produced the First World War and its aftermath, dada said that if reason, intellect, and morality could produce nothing better than a world of destruction, cruelty, and chaos, then there was no point in trying any longer to be reasonable, intellectual, or moral.

As a purely nihilistic movement dada was interesting as a phenomenon, no matter how disturbing this phenomenon was. But it turned out to have its own perverse logic. The "spontaneous" nature of dadaist creation made it an expression of the unconscious mind, according to developments in psychiatry at that time. Its nonsense sometimes did resemble nightmares, and it became meaningful in terms of the unconscious. Artists then became interested in exploring a world of irrational fantasy, in making a conscious investigation of the unconscious. Thus the spirit of dada developed into a school of fantasy with a program—surrealism.

Surrealism

Paradox is a large element in surrealism. Its dream forms are reproduced in paradoxically realistic detail; reality and unreality not only become confused with one another but they replace each other. The many expressions of this replacement of one world by another include the double image, as we have seen in Dali's *Apparition of Face and Fruit Dish on a Beach* (Portfolio 12, Plate 137). But earlier than this, Giorgio de Chirico (born 1888) had created, without benefit of surrealist theory, his dreamlike cityscapes in which bright but mysterious light illuminates the familiar yet irrational architecture of desolate squares with lonely vistas stretching into abruptly terminated distances (*Figure 22*). The surrealists claim Chirico as an ancestor, rightly, and Chagall is also called protosurrealist by some critics in spite of the great difference in spirit between the two artists.

Out of pure surrealism grew magic realism, a more flexible approach that sometimes shared surrealism's interest in dreams and expressed its visions in the same sharp detail. Magic realism, however, was not so often concerned with the hints—or outright statements—of morbidity that preoccupied the surrealists. It tended frequently to be theatrical in its effects—as in *Muse of the Western World* (*Figure 23*) by Eugene Berman (born 1899). On the other hand, magic realism could go so far in the other direction that even Wyeth's *River Cove* can be forced into the relation, at least, of a cousin to the movement.

The world of reverie, of nightmare, of enchantment, could hardly fail to find its expression in abstraction in a century so very much interested in exploring the possibilities of nonrepresentational art. And so we have yet another turnabout: surrealism, beginning as the least abstract of arts and precisely defined as such, itself produced its abstractionists. Joan Miró (born 1893), the leading contemporary fantasist in the opinion of most critics today, falls somewhere in between abstract and figurative surrealism, with his partly witty and partly frightening concoctions such as *Painting* (*Figure 24*). It is possible to find resemblances to bones, insects, and curious little animals in these forms, but they take on their fullest power when they are regarded as hallucina-

Figure 23

tions in which the rather entertaining character of the resemblances to things known is overpowered by their sinister transformation into forms that carry the terror of the unknown.

Still more abstract, although its title finally reveals its connection with identifiable forms, is *Moby Dick* (*Figure 25*) by William Baziotes (born 1912).

And finally we come, as in any discussion of contemporary art we must come again and again, back to Picasso. His *Head* (Plate L 12) demonstrates that of the infinite variations and combinations and recombinations of the forces that have determined the look of modern art, none can be isolated for long.

Head would never have been painted if Picasso's cubist experiments had not supplied a vocabulary of angular forms in which vestigial bits of nature remain identifiable. Yet to call the painting cubist is to stretch the definition of cubism to extreme limits. To call *Head* surrealist is also to abandon a definition, or to expand it beyond the early surrealist

27

Figure 24

principle of precise and tangible forms, no matter in what irrational combinations.

The forms nevertheless have the quality of fantastic invention, with some of the overtones of the violent or the sinister that we associate with surrealism. In addition, the picture has another quality whose presence may seem impossible to anyone who in the first place has trouble in accepting its abstract approach and then its eeriness: it has wit.

A dictionary defines wit as "the ability to make clever, ironic, or satirical remarks, usually by perceiving the incongruous and expressing it in a surprising or epigrammatic manner." Certainly *Head* is clever; Picasso is a master of legerdemain, and the vast quantity of his work (he is as productive an artist as

ever lived) includes examples that are a playful juggling of forms and ideas that have served him in more profound ways elsewhere. In its assurance, its deftness, *Head* has some of this quality, although whether there is anything "ironic or satirical" in it is a question that the individual must answer for himself. Picasso rarely explains the meaning of a picture or comments on his reasons for working in one way or another—quite rightly, since, as he says, he would write a book instead of painting a picture if what he expresses in paint he could better express in words.

A painting like *Head* is not one that can be pinned down and dissected to reveal every factor that went into its creation. Up to a certain point, yes; after that, the more we try

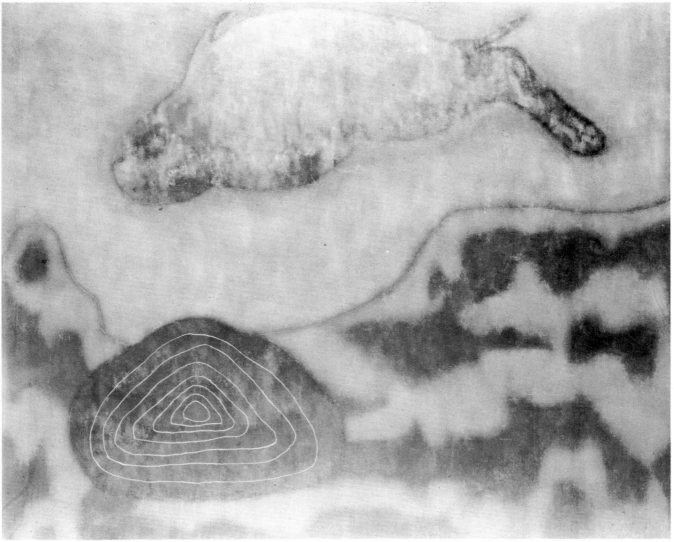

Figure 25

to explain, the greater danger we run of distorting the picture by crystallizing into words ideas that simply do not adapt themselves to verbal statement. Also, the person doing the explaining must do so from a point of view peculiar to himself and may thus block the observer from reaching his own conclusions through a personal response. The critic's job is to analyze a work of art as thoroughly as he can where objective analysis is possible; after that, if he offers an opinion (as has been done again and again in these discussions, of course) he must do so without pretensions to infallibility. Thus when we say that *Head* has cubist and surrealist connections we are safe enough; when we begin to talk about its "wit"

we are not quite so safe, although it seems extremely witty to this writer; if we go much beyond that, we are offering the kind of opinion or response that should be accepted for discussion rather than as dogma. For that reason these portfolios have been called "Seminars"—a seminar being a course of supervised study in which each member of the group takes part.

The reader has taken part silently, and often no doubt with great patience, but let us hope that, all in all, these rather one-sided discussions have shown some helpful ways of looking at art, and have suggested the infinite width and depth of material that the reader may now explore for himself.

Color Plates

Figures in the Text

18. LANDSCAPE WITH BLUEBIRDS, 1919, by Paul Klee (1879–1940), Swiss

Gouache on paper. Height 8″. The Philadelphia Museum of Art, A. E. Gallatin Collection

19. LETTER GHOST, 1937, by Paul Klee (1879–1940), Swiss

Gouache on newspaper. Height 13″. The Museum of Modern Art, New York, Mrs. John D. Rockefeller, Jr., Purchase Fund

20. THE POET, OR HALF PAST THREE, 1911, by Marc Chagall (born 1889), Russian

Oil on canvas. Height 6′ 5½″. The Philadelphia Museum of Art, Louise and Walter Arensberg Collection

21. WHY NOT SNEEZE, ROSE SÉLAVY, 1921, by Marcel Duchamp (born 1887), French

Marble blocks, thermometer, wood, and cuttlebone in small bird cage. Height 4½″. The Philadelphia Museum of Art, Louise and Walter Arensberg Collection

22. GARE MONTPARNASSE (THE MELANCHOLY OF DEPARTURE), 1914, by Giorgio de Chirico (born 1888), Italian

Oil on canvas. Height 55″. James Thrall Soby, New Canaan

23. MUSE OF THE WESTERN WORLD, 1942, by Eugene Berman (born 1899), American

Oil on canvas. Height 50⅞″. The Metropolitan Museum of Art, George A. Hearn Fund, 1943

24. PAINTING, 1933, by Joan Miró (born 1893), Spanish

Oil on canvas. Height 51.″ The Philadelphia Museum of Art, A. E. Gallatin Collection

25. MOBY DICK, 1955, by William Baziotes (born 1912), American

Oil on canvas. Height 60″. William A. M. Burden, New York